KAREEM ABDUL-JABBAR

PHOTO CREDITS
Carl Skalak, Jr.: pp. 9, 13, 17, 21, 29, and cover
Ronald C. Modra: pp. 5, 7, 23, 27, 31
Peter Travers: pp. 11, 15, 19
Bruce Curtis: p. 25

Published by Creative Educational Society, Inc.,
123 South Broad Street, Mankato, Minnesota 56001

Library of Congress Cataloging in Publication Data
Taylor, Paula.
Basketball's finest center, Kareem Abdul-Jabbar.
SUMMARY: A brief biography of the tall, black basketball player
who has won many honors in that sport.
1. Abdul-Jabbar, Kareem, 1947-   —Juvenile literature.
2. Basketball players—United States—Biography—Juvenile literature.
[1. Abdul-Jabbar, Kareem, 1947-   2. Basketball players] I. Title.
GV884.A24T38   796.32'3'0924 [B] [92]   76-45194   ISBN 0-87191-584-7

BASKETBALL'S FINEST CENTER KAREEM ABDUL-JABBAR

BY PAULA TAYLOR

CREATIVE EDUCATION/CHILDRENS PRESS

4

Opposing players feel helpless when they see
Kareem Abdul-Jabbar coming. How do you guard
someone who's so tall you have to tilt your head back
to look him in the eye? — Someone whose hands are
so big they can grasp a basketball the way most
people grab a grapefruit? — Someone who can jump
up and snatch a 12-foot high pass out of thin air?

6

Being 7'1⅜" tall gives Jabbar a big advantage on the basketball court. But Kareem Abdul-Jabbar hasn't become the finest center in the game because of his height alone.

Jabbar passes accurately and dribbles with lightning speed. He shoots either right or left-handed. He can stuff a shot from as far away as the free throw line.

8

Jabbar's many talents put him smack in the center of the action. When he moves, the other players follow him. When he stands still, everyone clusters around him. Opposing guards can't afford to let Jabbar get free, even for a second. He averages over 30 points a game!

10

"You practically have to smash Jabbar in the mouth before he gets aggressive," Kareem's UCLA coach once said.

Getting used to the pro's rough style of play was hard for Kareem at first. During his first pro season with the Milwaukee Bucks he took a lot of bruising punches. It took a long time before he got angry enough to hit back.

Now Jabbar wrestles for position like everybody else, but he still gets tired of the pushing and shoving. He feels that basketball should be a game of skill, not a contact sport.

12

When Jabbar fouls, the crowd sometimes boos him, but he rarely gets angry. He just stands with his hands on his hips and stares back at the hecklers. When people are cheering him, his expression isn't much different.

14

Jabbar rarely smiles. Sportswriters and fans have accused him of being cold and unfeeling, but Kareem says that's not true.

"I have a hyperactive mind," he says. "I have to clear my mind to play basketball. I can't have it all cluttered. That's why I look relaxed. But I'm not relaxed. I'm all worked up, man, deep down inside."

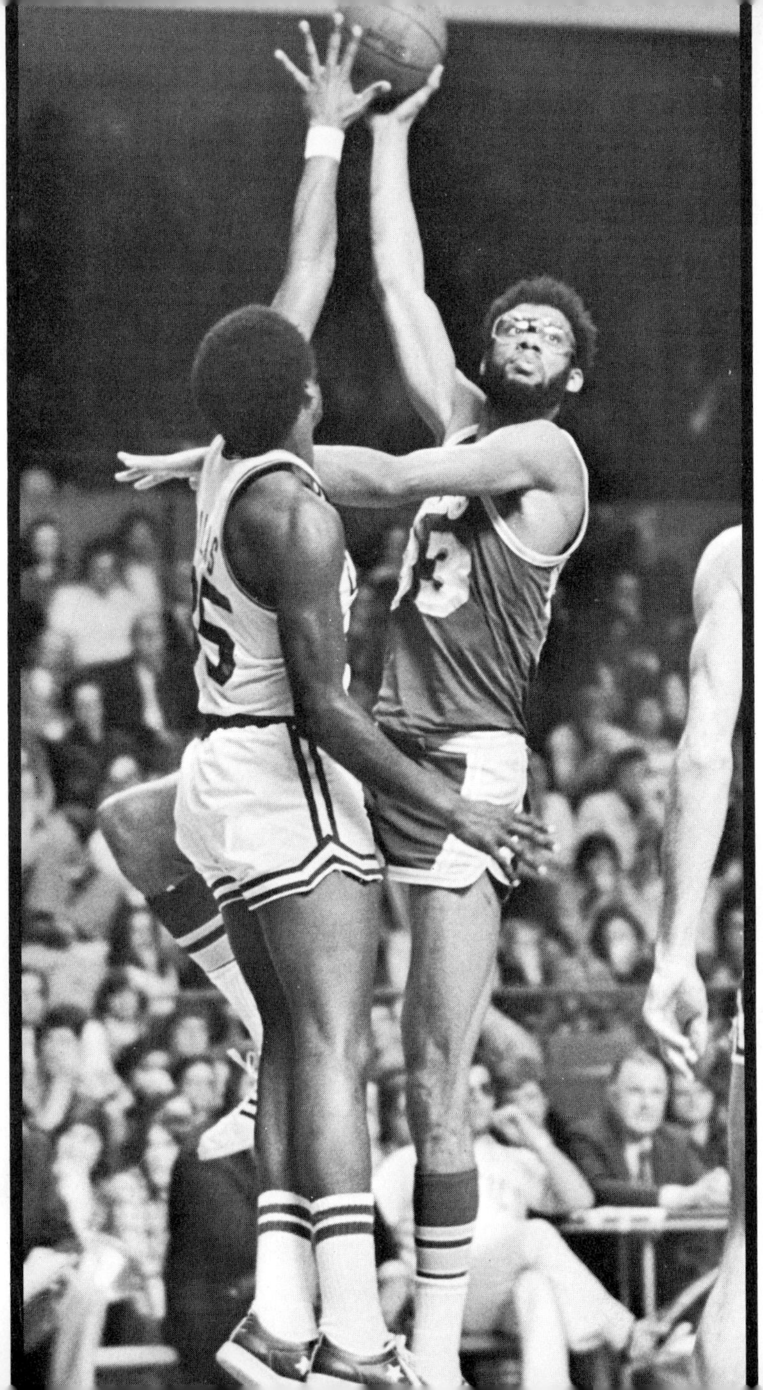

16

Jabbar usually ambles onto the court, chewing a wad of Juicy Fruit gum. While the "Star Spangled Banner" is being played, he stares sleepily up at the rafters. He looks bored, but he's not. He's concentrating. Sometimes Jabbar plays with such total concentration that he seems to be off in a world of his own.

18

When Jabbar hurls one of his sky hooks toward the net, his eyes have a far-away look. He seems detached from the action around him.

At home Kareem also likes being in his private world. He spends a lot of time alone, reading or listening to music.

On buses or planes he often throws his coat over his head and goes to sleep or listens to modern jazz on his portable tape recorder.

"Loneliness is good," says Jabbar, "because it means privacy, which is most important of all to me."

"Ever since childhood I had this ability to withdraw into myself," Kareem says. "I had to. I was always a minority of one."

Kareem was always different: a Catholic . . . taller than anyone else . . . one of a handful of black kids in the neighborhood . . . one of two black kids at his grade school.

Kareem's parents taught him not to be afraid of being different. "Stand tall," his father told him.

Kareem grew up, proud of his Nigerian grandfather, who spoke Yoruba. He was proud of his grandmother, who came from Trinidad and had a musical way of speaking.

22

But slowly Kareem realized that he wasn't treated the same as his neighbors, whose grandparents came from Ireland or Russia.

His white neighbors could go to the barber down the block. But Kareem and his father had to take the bus all the way to Harlem to get their hair cut.

For a while Kareem and a white boy named John were best friends, but suddenly John couldn't play any more.

By the time Kareem was in high school, he felt there was a wall separating him from his white teachers and classmates.

"'I wish you didn't have any white in you at all," he told his mother bitterly, "because I hate every drop of white blood I have in me."

24

For years afterwards Kareem struggled with his angry feelings. He wanted to fight back . . . to throw a garbage can through a store window . . . to hurt someone.

But he didn't. He read a lot of books, and he thought a lot. "What's wrong with being black?" he kept wondering.

At last he found the answer. There was nothing wrong with being black — or white, or tall, or short; but it was wrong to hate anyone for being any of these.

Kareem found his answer in Islam. He decided to become a Muslim. Ever since that time he's worn a gold chain around his neck. On the chain is the star and crescent of Islam.

26

Before Kareem became a Muslim, his name was Lew Alcindor. When Kareem changed his religion, he took an Islamic name. Kareem Abdul-Jabbar means "generous and powerful servant of God." It took a while for Kareem's family and friends to get used to his new name. Basketball announcers and fans got mixed up too, but now hardly anybody calls him Lew Alcindor any more.

Jabbar has won his share of honors. He's been the league's leading scorer and most valuable player. He's been on the NBA's All Star Team.

He's also made a lot of money. But the big money hasn't changed Jabbar much.

After signing his first pro contract, Kareem went on a spending spree. He bought some new jeans because the old ones had holes. He bought a Cadillac because his legs got cramped in his old car, and he bought a set of drums because he'd always wanted to play the drums.

"Basketball has been a pretty good part of my life," says Jabbar, "but basketball isn't everything."

When Kareem was in college, he spent his summers trying to encourage poor black kids to stay in school and off drugs. One summer Kareem could have played in the Olympics. But he felt working with kids was more important than winning a gold medal. So he stayed home.

Kareem Abdul-Jabbar doesn't want to be thought of as just a basketball star. He is determined to live up to the name he has chosen for himself.

BILLIE JEAN KING
O. J. SIMPSON
EVEL KNIEVEL
HANK AARON
JOE NAMATH
OLGA KORBUT
FRAN TARKENTON
MUHAMMAD ALI
CHRIS EVERT
FRANCO HARRIS
BOBBY ORR
KAREEM ABDUL JABBAR
JACK NICKLAUS
JOHNNY BENCH
JIMMY CONNORS
A. J. FOYT

THE ALLSTARS